SandCastle 3

Vowel Blends

ea

Mary Elizabeth Salzmann

Published by SandCastle™, an imprint of ABDO Publishing Company, 4940 Viking Drive, Edina, Minnesota 55435.

Printed in the United States.

Cover and interior photo credits: Eyewire Images, PhotoDisc

Library of Congress Cataloging-in-Publication Data

Salzmann, Mary Elizabeth, 1968-
    Ea / Mary Elizabeth Salzmann.
    p. cm. -- (Vowel blends)
    ISBN 1-57765-454-4
    1. Readers (Primary) [1. Readers.] I. Title.

PE1119 .S234216 2001
428.1--dc21

00-056560

The SandCastle concept, content, and reading method have been reviewed and approved by a national advisory board including literacy specialists, librarians, elementary school teachers, early childhood education professionals, and parents.

Let Us Know

After reading the book, SandCastle would like you to tell us your stories about reading. What is your favorite page? Was there something hard that you needed help with? Share the ups and downs of learning to read. We want to hear from you! To get posted on the ABDO Publishing Company Web site, send us email at:

sandcastle@abdopub.com

About SandCastle™

Nonfiction books for the beginning reader

- Basic concepts of phonics are incorporated with integrated language methods of reading instruction. Most words are short, and phrases, letter sounds, and word sounds are repeated.

- Readability is determined by the number of words in each sentence, the number of characters in each word, and word lists based on curriculum frameworks.

- Full-color photography reinforces word meanings and concepts.

- "Words I Can Read" list at the end of each book teaches basic elements of grammar, helps the reader recognize the words in the text, and builds vocabulary.

- Reading levels are indicated by the number of flags on the castle.

Look for more SandCastle books in these three reading levels:

Level 1 (one flag)	Level 2 (two flags)	Level 3 (three flags)
Grades Pre-K to K	**Grades K to 1**	**Grades 1 to 2**
5 or fewer words per page	5 to 10 words per page	10 to 15 words per page

Dean and his dad appear
to have fun in the fall
leaves.

Jean likes to read with her mom.

They read a book each day.

7

ea

Jeanie and Meara are
making many neat things
with beads.

9

ea

Neal giggles and squeals
when his mom tickles
his ear.

Meagan and Reagan help build a big sand castle at the beach.

Teagan can hear the sea when she holds this shell near her ear.

Keane likes to fish in the stream.

His dad will clean the fish he catches.

Keanan steals second base during his Little League game.

He slides in safely.

19

Keagan has a yummy treat.

What is he eating?

(ice cream)

Words I Can Read

Nouns

A noun is a person, place, or thing

base (BAYSS) p. 19
beach (BEECH) p. 13
beads (BEEDZ) p. 9
book (BUK) p. 7
dad (DAD) pp. 5, 17
day (DAY) p. 7
ear (IHR) pp. 11, 15

fish (FISH) p. 17
fun (FUHN) p. 5
game (GAME) p. 19
ice cream (EYESS KREEM) p. 21
leaves (LEEVZ) p. 5
mom (MOM) pp. 7, 11

sand castle (SAND KASS-uhl) p. 13
sea (SEE) p. 15
shell (SHEL) p. 15
stream (STREEM) p. 17
things (THINGZ) p. 9
treat (TREET) p. 21

Proper Nouns

A proper noun is the name
of a person, place, or thing

Dean (DEEN) p. 5
Jean (JEEN) p. 7
Jeanie (JEE-nee) p. 9
Keagan (KEE-guhn) p. 21

Keanan (KEE-nuhn) p. 19
Keane (KEEN) p. 17
Meagan (MEE-guhn) p. 13
Meara (MEE-ruh) p. 9

Neal (NEEL) p. 11
Reagan (REE-guhn) p. 13
Teagan (TEE-guhn) p. 15

Pronouns

A pronoun is a word that replaces a noun

he (HEE) pp. 17, 19, 21
she (SHEE) p. 15

they (THAY) p. 7

what (WUHT) p. 21

22

Verbs
A verb is an action or being word

appear (uh-PIHR) p. 5
are (AR) p. 9
build (BILD) p. 13
can (KAN) p. 15
catches (KA-chez) p. 17
clean (KLEEN) p. 17
eating (EET-ing) p. 21
fish (FISH) p. 17

giggles (GIG-uhlz) p. 11
has (HAZ) p. 21
have (HAV) p. 5
hear (HIHR) p. 15
help (HELP) p. 13
holds (HOHLDZ) p. 15
is (IZ) p. 21
likes (LIKESS) pp. 7, 17

making (MAKE-ing) p. 9
read (REED) p. 7
slides (SLIDEZ) p. 19
squeals (SKWEELZ) p. 11
steals (STEELZ) p. 19
tickles (TIK-uhlz) p. 11
will (WIL) p. 17

Adjectives
An adjective describes something

big (BIG) p. 13
each (EECH) p. 7
fall (FAWL) p. 5
her (HUR) pp. 7, 15

his (HIZ) pp. 5, 11, 17, 19
Little League (LIT-uhl LEEG) p. 19
many (MEN-ee) p. 9
neat (NEET) p. 9

second (SEK-uhnd) p. 19
this (THISS) p. 15
yummy (YUHM-ee) p. 21

Adverbs
An adverb tells how, when, or where something happens

safely (SAYF-lee) p. 19

Glossary

beads – Small pieces of glass, wood, or plastic with holes for string to pass through.

Little League – A group of baseball teams for children.

stream – A body of flowing water, such as a brook or small river.

More ea Words

beat	feast	please
beaver	gleam	real
dear	heat	seal
dream	jeans	teach
eagle	lead	wheat
east	mean	year